War Secrets

Jane Wood

TOP SECRET

Some people just can't help giving a secret away. Others can keep a secret as though their life depended on it. In the Second World War, that's just what happened: **people's lives depended on secrets**. People had to keep many different kinds of secrets. Some people worked in secret places that the enemy didn't know about. Some people intercepted secret messages. Others had to live secretly in order to survive.

In each section of this book, you'll find a secret word written in code. Write down each code and then use the code breaker on page 48 to work out the message.

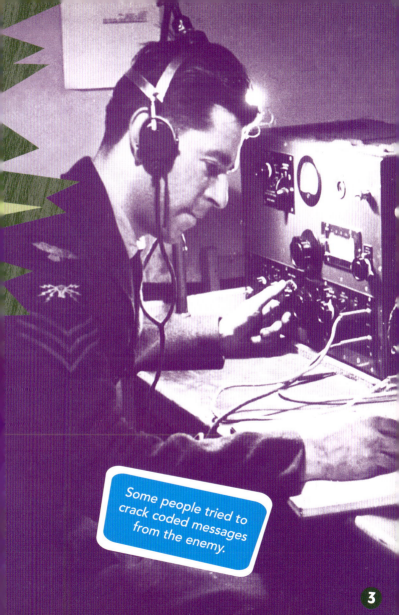

Some people tried to crack coded messages from the enemy.

TOP SECRET DOCUMENTS

The Secret Bomb Store

Find out why Britain's biggest explosion was kept secret!

PAGES 6 TO 13

Put your thinking cap on as we meet the clever code breakers!

PAGES 14 TO 23

Enigma: The Secret Code

The Secret Army of Animals!

It wasn't just humans who were war heroes!

A Secret Home

Could you live in secret for nearly two years?

The Resistance

Find out how children helped this secret organisation fight the war...

The Secret Bomb Store

In the Second World War, there was an enormous explosion in Britain. It was the third biggest explosion of the whole war, anywhere in the world. But most people have never heard about it! What's more, it wasn't caused by enemy bombing – it was an **accident!**

The explosion happened on 27th November 1944, at a secret weapons storage depot in a quiet part of the countryside in the Midlands. The storage depot was in a disused mine at Fauld, in Staffordshire. The government thought that the explosives could be kept safely there …

"It looked like an Aladdin's cave. You went from one cavern to another, by passages ablaze with electric light. In the caverns, the lighting had an eerie effect, and in the dark caves, you could see faintly, the tiers of enormous high explosive bombs."

(Officer, quoted in a report in The Burton Observer & Chronicle, Thursday 30 November 1944)

The underground tunnels in the mine were big enough to drive lorries through and had earth ceilings nearly 30 metres thick!

It was the biggest man-made explosion that Britain has ever seen.

What triggered the explosion? Witnesses saw two airmen working on **faulty live bombs**, with their detonators still in place. This kind of work was forbidden because it was too dangerous. Somehow, something went wrong. First, a single bomb blew up. The impact from the rush of air then set off more than 3,500 tons of bombs, all at once!

EYEWITNESS
I was there!

"The first was like an ordinary 500-pounder going off, and I was not too worried. Then came the second explosion. Along the tunnel in front I could see a cloud of dust coming towards me. Then the lights went out, and the suction from the gigantic explosion bashed me out of the office."

(Joseph Clifford Salt, quoted in The Burton Observer & Chronicle, Thursday 30 November 1944)

The explosion threw millions of tons of earth high into the air. A pair of huge mushroom clouds of dust and rubble rose into the sky and could be seen for miles around. Rescuers tried to find survivors, but it was very difficult. The tunnels were full of poisonous gas and debris from the explosion. Water from a nearby reservoir flooded through the broken ground into the tunnels, making the search even harder.

The explosion left a crater about half a mile across and 90 metres deep.

"There was just one tremendous roar. The horizon itself seemed to have altered. The whole face of the landscape was different. I found it difficult to get my bearings."

(Joseph Foster, quoted in the Daily Herald, 1958)

FaR FLuNG FaCT

The blast was heard 19 miles away, and the shock registered as an earth tremor in Geneva, Switzerland and Casablanca, North Africa.

OOhh! Milk-Shake!

The Blast was Britain's Biggest EXPLOSION.

Sadly, 68 people lost their lives.

Your first code to bre

Yet even today, not many people know about it. Why? Well, during the war the government were careful not to let people know about things that might lower morale. Also, the government didn't want the enemy to know about any problems it had. So the disaster at Fauld was hardly reported in the news, at the time. It's only more recently that people have finally begun to hear about what happened there.

If you visit Fauld today, you can see memorials to the people who lost their lives, and read about what happened.

Enigma:
The Secret Code

Codes and ciphers have always been important for passing on secret messages. During the Second World War, many people worked hard at making codes that no one would be able to understand. At the same time, many more people worked hard at trying to 'break' those codes.

The Nazis used a complicated machine called the 'Enigma' to code their messages.

The Nazis needed to send secret messages to plan their battle action. The messages had to be sent by radio using Morse code. Anyone with a suitable receiver can pick up radio messages, so the messages had to be in a code that no one else would understand …

The Enigma machine contained several wheels, each with the alphabet written round the edge. The letters on the wheels were connected up so that when you typed in a letter, a different code letter would be produced. To make it even more difficult, every time you pressed a letter on the keyboard, one of the disks would move round, changing the code. So every letter of every message was coded using a slightly different system!

Not only did the code change with every letter, but the connections that scrambled the letters were altered every day. So even if you found the solution one day, it would only work up until midnight!

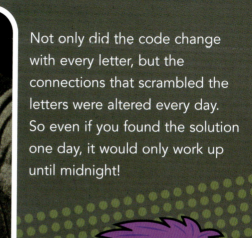

There were lots of possible combinations ... **150 million million million** possible combinations, to be precise! So it was pretty impossible just to guess the right solution.

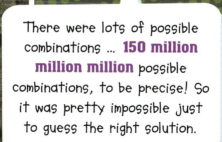

In Britain, a secret code-breaking headquarters was set up. Its code name was Station X. Winston Churchill, the prime minister, called it his 'ultra secret'. Everyone who worked at Station X had to sign the **Official Secrets Act** and promise never to talk about their work.

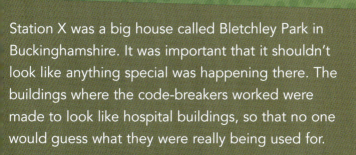

Station X was a big house called Bletchley Park in Buckinghamshire. It was important that it shouldn't look like anything special was happening there. The buildings where the code-breakers worked were made to look like hospital buildings, so that no one would guess what they were really being used for.

the Enigma code was broken

But everything at Station X was so secret that only a handful of people in all of Station X knew about this momentous breakthrough. The secrecy didn't end there ... Once the code had been broken, Station X was able to tell the authorities what the Nazis were planning. However, the work of Station X was so secret that even the British generals didn't know where the secret information was coming from, and they didn't realise it was true. So at first they ignored it!

CRacked it!

er... my pencil ...that is!

A team of brilliant mathematicians worked as code-breakers at Bletchley Park.

Once the intelligence from Station X was taken seriously, the British government had to hide the fact that the Enigma code had been broken. They pretended they were getting their secret information from a spy codenamed 'Boniface'. **Why?** Britain needed the Nazis to think that there was a spy, so they wouldn't realise that anyone had broken the code of their secret messages.

Even today, Bletchley Park has got its secrets. The people who work there still aren't sure of all their facts about it. There are still a lot of secrets that no one has ever told ...

Bletchley Park has been called Britain's best-kept secret. A film called **Enigma** was made in 2000 and tells the story of the Station X code-breakers.

The Secret Army of Animals!

The Dickin Medal is the 'animal Victoria Cross'. It is awarded for outstanding devotion to duty by an animal working for a military unit. The award was created in 1943 by Maria Dickin, the founder of the PDSA (People's Dispensary for Sick Animals). Are you ready to meet three award-winning war heroes?

I flew faster than G.I. Joe, you know!

In the Second World War, 32 pigeons received the Dickin Medal for their work!

G.I. Joe

Top secret war messenger

G.I. Joe was a pigeon who worked as a secret messenger. He won the Dickin Medal for flying 20 miles in 20 minutes to deliver a vital message. That's an average speed of 60 miles an hour! He delivered the message just in time to prevent around 100 soldiers from being bombed by their own planes. This mission was described as 'the most outstanding flight by a USA Army Pigeon in World War II'.

Frankenstein the Cat

Reporting for duties aboard HMS Belfast

In the 1940s, HMS **Belfast** carried a cat called Frankenstein. Her job was to catch rats and mice on the ship, so that they couldn't damage any equipment or steal and spoil the food supplies. She was also a pet for the men on board – having a cat to care for helped them to keep their spirits up. War didn't seem to bother Frankenstein. On 26th December 1943, HMS **Belfast** was involved in the Battle of North Cape, a nine-hour attack on a German battleship. Frankenstein slept through the whole thing!

CODED MESSAGE Your third code to bre

Gander the Dog

Life-saving rescue worker with the Royal Rifles of Canada

Gander, a Newfoundland dog, saved the lives of a group of wounded Canadian soldiers in Hong Kong in 1941. He barked and snapped at enemy troops, forcing them to retreat. Then he saw that a live grenade had landed near the soldiers. He picked it up in his mouth and carried it away from them. It exploded and killed him instantly. The Dickin Medal was awarded to the memory of Gander in 2000, nearly 60 years after his heroic actions.

A Secret Home

During the Second World War, many people's safety depended on keeping secrets. In Germany, the Nazis persecuted Jewish people. They rounded up thousands of Jews and sent them away to concentration camps. Many Jews died in these camps. Some saw the danger coming, and ran away or hid before the Nazis could arrest them. Anne Frank and her family were Jewish. They moved from Germany to Holland to escape from the Nazis. But when the Nazis took over Holland, the Frank family knew they were in danger, so they went into hiding.

FRaNK FaCT

Anne Frank's diary was published after the war and is now famous all over the world. It has been published in more than 55 languages and has become one of the most widely read books in the world.

world Best Seller!

Today, we know what happened to the Frank family because Anne Frank wrote a diary while she was in hiding. Anne was just 13 years old when she went into hiding.

The hiding place was a flat at the top of the building where Anne's father ran his business.

Anne's father prepared a secret hiding place for his family. He took some furniture, bedding, clothes, and whatever dried and tinned food he could get. He kept his plans secret even from his daughters. Anne had no idea about the preparations her father was making. Then one day, a letter came ordering her sister to report to the Nazis for work. Mr Frank knew it was time to hide. He told the family what his secret plan was. Quickly, they gathered up a few things, put on as many clothes as they could manage, and went to the hiding place.

EYEWITNESS
I was there!

"I don't think I'll ever feel at home in this house, but that doesn't mean I hate it. It may be damp and lopsided, but there's probably not a more comfortable hiding place in all of Amsterdam."

(Anne Frank's diary, 11 July 1942)

Anne called the hiding place 'the Secret Annexe', because the entrance was hidden behind a heavy bookcase. The Frank family and their friends, the van Daan family, lived in six small rooms for nearly **two years, without leaving the building!** They passed the time by talking, reading, playing games and doing exercises. And Anne wrote her diary. Just a few close and trusted friends knew they were there. They brought food to them secretly, and told them what was happening in the outside world.

EYEWITNESS
I was there!

"If you have been shut up for a year and a half, it can get to be too much for you sometimes. I long to ride a bike, dance, whistle, look at the world, feel young and know that I'm free, and yet I can't let it show."

(Anne Frank's diary, 24 December 1943)

A movable bookcase was built to hide the stairs leading to the Secret Annexe.

During the day, the building where the Frank family was hiding was still in use as a warehouse. Everyone in the Secret Annexe had to be very quiet. They couldn't move about or talk. They took care not to use any water or switch the lights on, in case anyone heard or saw anything, too. Anne was a lively, chatty person. She found it very hard to keep still and stay quiet all day. She often felt irritated by the other people, especially by her mother and Mrs van Daan, who always seemed to be telling her off.

EYEWITNESS
I was there!

"Not being able to go outside upsets me more than I can say, and I'm terrified our hiding place will be discovered and that we'll be shot."

(Anne Frank's diary, 28 September 1942)

> Anne let off steam by writing her feelings in her diary.

Anne kept the diary in a secret place so the others couldn't read it. Once, Mrs van Daan asked if she could read the page Anne had just finished. Anne said no. Later she wrote: "I nearly died, since that particular page contained a rather unflattering description of her." (Anne Frank's diary, 21 September 1942)

On 4th August 1944,

the Frank Family were discovered ...

... and taken away to concentration camps.

Someone must have seen or heard something, and given their secret away. The police came and searched the house. While Anne and her family kept absolutely quiet, the police examined the building in detail. Finally, the police discovered the entrance behind the bookcase. They found the way up to the Secret Annexe and arrested Anne's family and their friends.

For Anne and the others, the betrayal of their secret was disastrous. After only a few months in the concentration camps, all of them, except for Anne's father, were dead

The Resistance

The Nazis took over many parts of Europe in the Second World War. The Nazis controlled everything, and tried to make everyone obey them. Many of the ordinary people who lived in these countries wanted to help defeat the Nazis. They joined secret organisations, known as the Resistance, to fight against them. Some helped soldiers who were lost and Jews who were in danger. Others acted as spies and passed on secret information.

They had to be very careful and very brave, because if the Nazis found out what they were doing, they would be punished, or maybe even shot.

The role of the Resistance in bringing down the Nazis is remembered today.

OU JE MEURS
RENAIT LA
PATRIE

ARAGON

AIN-HAUT-JURA
AUX MORTS DES MAQUIS
ET DE LA RÉSISTANCE

Marcel Marceau was a young boy during the war. He grew up in a town in France. When the Nazis took over his town, they tried to send all the Jewish people to the concentration camps in Germany. Marcel and his brother ran away to another town. They changed their names so that no one would guess that they were really Jewish.

EYEWITNESS
I was there!

"For two months I was hidden by a wonderful woman who hid in her institute, during the wartime, 90 children who were Jewish among 100 Gentile children, side by side. If somebody would have gone to the Gestapo or the French Militia, who were fascists, everybody would have been deported."

(Marcel Marceau, quoted in an acceptance speech for an award given to him for his life's work.)

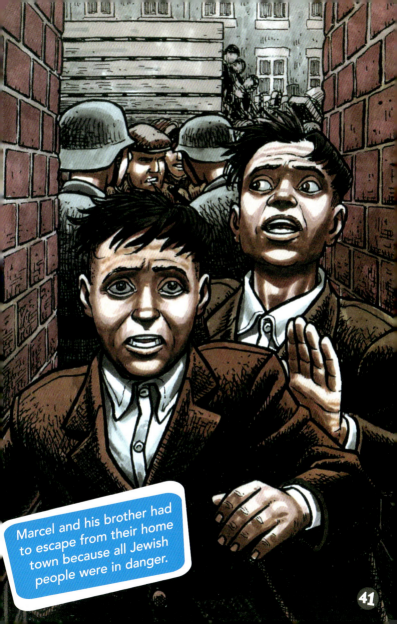

Marcel and his brother had to escape from their home town because all Jewish people were in danger.

In France, these 'Cartes D'Identité' were often checked at railway stations.

As soon as he could, Marcel joined the Resistance movement. He helped other young people to escape from the Nazis. Marcel was a boy scout. He knew how to travel through the mountains safely, without being seen. He guided children who were in danger through the mountains from France to Switzerland, where they would be safe.

Marcel was good at art. He used his skills to change people's identity photos so they would look younger than they really were. This meant that they would seem too young to be sent away to work in Germany.

FaMouS FaCT

When he grew up, Marcel Marceau became a famous mime artist. The characters he creates often have a sad feeling about them. Some people think that this is because he wants to make the audience think about how terrible war is, and how sad it makes people.

In 2003, 77-year-old Marguerite Garden, of Lanark, Scotland, received an award from the French government for her work as a schoolgirl spy during the war – 60 years after the event! Marguerite grew up in France. When she was 14, she and her parents joined the Resistance and helped airmen to escape back to Britain. They also set up a secret radio, which a trained operator used to send information to Britain.

One day, Marguerite noticed a tower in a field and asked the farmer what it was for. He told her that it was for talking to submarines. He didn't realise that she was a spy because she was just a child. The radio operator sent Marguerite's information to Station X, at Bletchley Park. In just a few days, the British airforce bombed the tower, to destroy the Nazis' communications system.

CODED MESSAGE

Your fifth and final

During term-time, Marguerite went to school in Paris, far away from her family. She looked like an ordinary schoolgirl, carrying an ordinary suitcase. In fact, it contained secret documents, which she took to another member of the Resistance in Paris. Eventually, the Nazis worked out that Marguerite's family were in the Resistance. Marguerite and her mother had to hide until the end of the war.

EYEWITNESS
I was there!

"I was at school in Paris and it took me three days to get home, but when I got there and saw the Germans in their uniforms I knew we had to fight them. It wasn't bravery, it was necessity. It was sad and frightening."

(Marguerite Garden, quoted in The Guardian, Friday 13 June 2003)

Well, now those war secrets have been uncovered, it's time to work out what all the coded messages mean, by using this code breaker. Find the letter of the code on the top row, and look up what letter it stands for on the bottom row. For example, MHI LXVKXM means TOP SECRET!

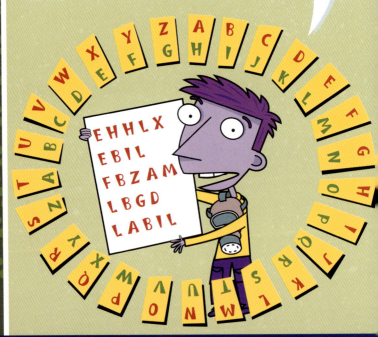